Boy Loves Girl, Girl Loves Boy

TEAR-AND-SEND POSTCARDS FOR FRIENDS AND LOVERS FROM THE GREAT ROMANCE COMIC BOOKS

Selected by Michael Barson

PANTHEON BOOKS NEW YORK

Love (sob!): a user's guide

LOVE

LOVE. It's a four-letter word—a puzzle that few of us have been able to solve for more than ten minutes. Why do we always get it wrong? Why didn't anyone ever hand us an operator's manual? If love is the drug, when can we take the cure?

Now, at long last, help is at hand. No, we don't mean "Oprah." Even *she* might learn something from *BOY LOVES GIRL, GIRL LOVES BOY*, this heart-stopping collection of 23 covers from the classic romance comic books of the 1940s and 1950s. Now you can absorb the hard-won lessons of love—representing many centuries of painful trial and error—in just a few seconds a day. Consider the moral implications of "I Flirted with Trouble." Gasp at the agony suffusing "Mother's Boy." Ponder the displaced personality of "I Was 'The Other Woman.'" Empathize with the humiliation of "Men Didn't Respect Me." Then take two aspirin and call us in the morning.

And there's more. Series editor Michael Barson, a man of vast emotional resources, has conscientiously selected key passages from each story to further illuminate the message at hand, for those of you too damaged to glean it on your own.

Yes, the utter disaster of what now passes for your love life can be transformed into unadulterated triumph with nothing more than the (shamefully modest) cost of this volume and a handful of 29¢ stamps. (Don't try to get away with using postcard stamps—the USPS will feed such undervalued examples to their summer interns and then return the mangled results with a smirk.)

It's a well-known fact that each of us has a potential soulmate lurking somewhere in the continental United States or its colonies. If you have the ability to detach one of the cards along the dotted line and to scrawl a simple message (remember, though: never beg!), eternal happiness is virtually guaranteed. Or quadruple your money back.

—*Dr. Michael Barson, Director,*
Research Institute of Young Loveology

BOY LOVES GIRL
DECEMBER
NO. 41 10¢
AUTHORIZED A. C. M. P.
CONFORMS to the COMICS CODE
PDC
I TELL YOU HE'S NO GOOD!
BUT I LOVE HIM!
LEV GLEASON INTEGRITY PUBLICATIONS

FROM BOY LOVES GIRL, GIRL LOVES BOY · PANTHEON BOOKS · ED. MICHAEL BARSON · COMPILATION AND NEW TEXT © 1992 BY MICHAEL BARSON

Boy Loves Girl #41 (1952)

"Did it ever occur to you, Helen, that you might have waited too long for Bob! You've been going with him for three years now—and your marriage is still not in sight! You're twenty-three now, Helen, going on twenty-four."

"I've heard this a hundred times! I'm waiting for Bob!"

"Three more years will go by and you still won't be married! You'll be much older then and your chances of getting a husband will be nil! You're making a mistake waiting for him. No man appreciates it! You're making a fool of yourself, Helen! And of your family!"

BOY LOVES GIRL
DECEMBER
NO. 41 10¢
AUTHORIZED A. C. M. P.
CONFORMS to the COMICS CODE
PDC
I TELL YOU HE'S NO GOOD!
BUT I LOVE HIM!
LEV GLEASON INTEGRITY PUBLICATIONS

FROM BOY LOVES GIRL, GIRL LOVES BOY · PANTHEON BOOKS · ED. MICHAEL BARSON · COMPILATION AND NEW TEXT © 1992 BY MICHAEL BARSON

Boy Loves Girl #41 (1952)

"Did it ever occur to you, Helen, that you might have waited too long for Bob! You've been going with him for three years now—and your marriage is still not in sight! You're twenty-three now, Helen, going on twenty-four."

"I've heard this a hundred times! I'm waiting for Bob!"

"Three more years will go by and you still won't be married! You'll be much older then and your chances of getting a husband will be nil! You're making a mistake waiting for him. No man appreciates it! You're making a fool of yourself, Helen! And of your family!"

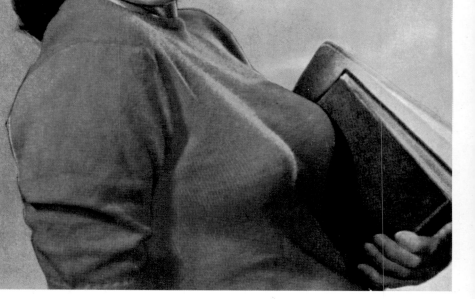

Hi-School
Romance

PDC

December
10¢

I HAD TO SHARE
MY BOY FRIEND

————————

LOVE ISN'T FUNNY

————————

MY PHANTOM LOVER

FROM BOY LOVES GIRL, GIRL LOVES BOY · PANTHEON BOOKS · ED. MICHAEL BARSON · COMPILATION AND NEW TEXT © 1992 BY MICHAEL BARSON

Hi-School Romance #2 (1949)

"Tom Tom! Oh! My Tom!"

Words are so useless when the one you love has you in his arms and presses his lips on yours! Words were not necessary anymore. We were in love, and we were together! Tom is returning to school this fall—to Standard University, where we will be seniors together—until graduation. Then we shall be married! College graduates then, but in life really freshmen . . . with the years before us and the stars in our eyes!

WARTIME
Romances

TRUE, ROMANTIC ADVENTURES IN THE ARMED SERVICES

ANC

BUT YOU CAN'T GO INTO THE ARMY NOW! THINK OF ME! WHAT WILL I DO? WE'VE INVESTED EVERY CENT WE HAVE IN THIS DINER.

YOU CAN RUN IT BY YOURSELF WITHOUT ANY TROUBLE IF YOU REMEMBER YOU'RE MARRIED AND JUST STOP FLIRTING WITH THE CUSTOMERS!

FRANKS AND BEANS 55¢

It's hard to be true when your sweetheart's overseas. It was even harder for me when I met Bob Simms...

I was sure I could make Jack forget his wife. She was in the States...we were in Germany with our own book of rules...

No. 7   TEN CENTS

FROM BOY LOVES GIRL, GIRL LOVES BOY · PANTHEON BOOKS · ED. MICHAEL BARSON · COMPILATION AND NEW TEXT © 1992 BY MICHAEL BARSON

Wartime Romances #7 (1952)

"What is it, Jack? Nothing wrong, I hope."

"It's a notice from my draft board. They want me to report for a physical."

"You can't go, Jack! You've got to get out of it! There must be a way! Can't you simulate a heart condition?"

"Nothing doing, Helen. I don't want to have anything to do with that kind of trickery!"

"You're a fool! There's nothing I wouldn't do if I were in your boots!"

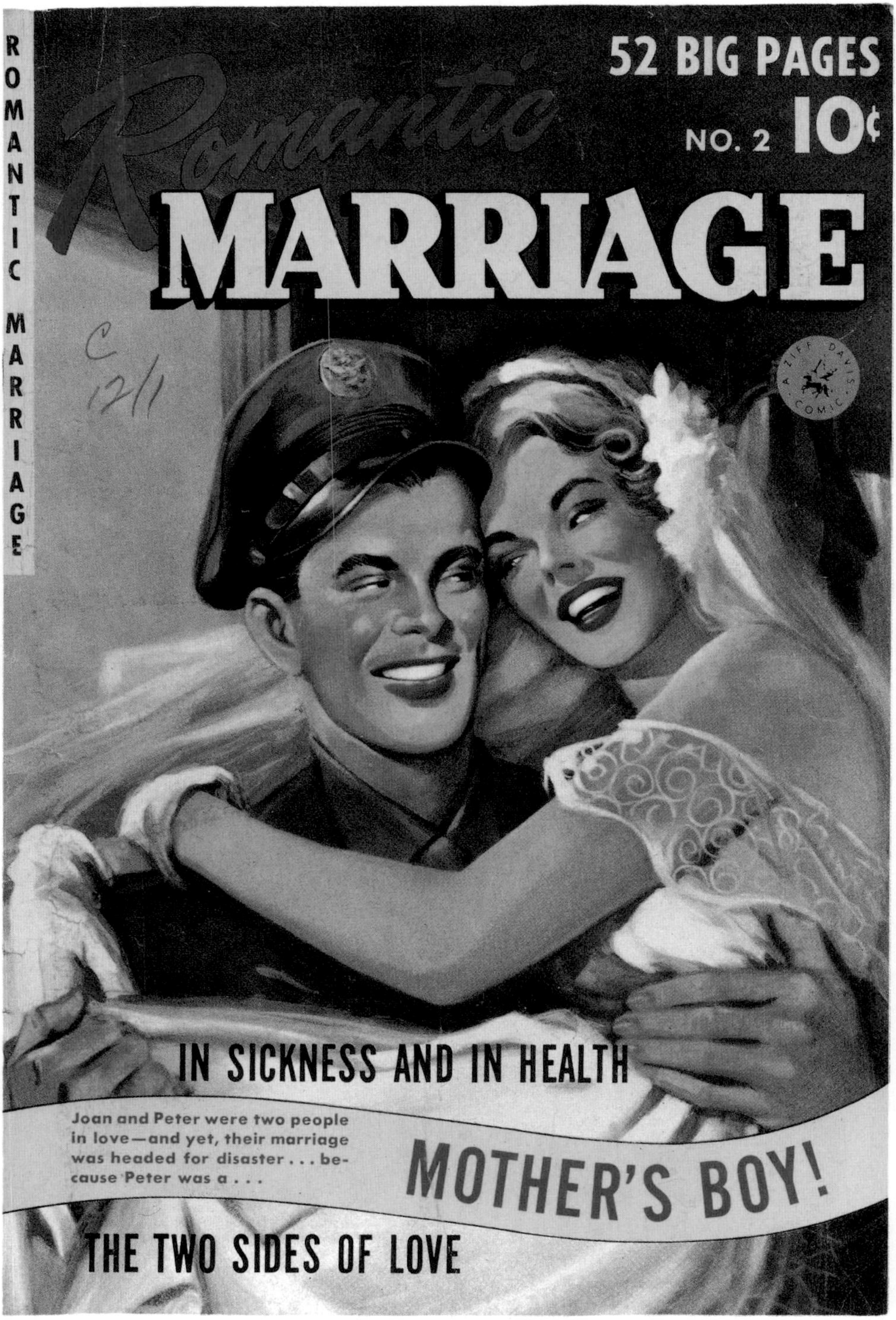
ROMANTIC MARRIAGE
52 BIG PAGES
Romantic
NO. 2
10¢
MARRIAGE
A ZIFF DAVIS COMIC
IN SICKNESS AND IN HEALTH
Joan and Peter were two people in love—and yet, their marriage was headed for disaster . . . because Peter was a . . .
MOTHER'S BOY!
THE TWO SIDES OF LOVE

FROM BOY LOVES GIRL, GIRL LOVES BOY · PANTHEON BOOKS · ED. MICHAEL BARSON · COMPILATION AND NEW TEXT © 1992 BY MICHAEL BARSON

Place First Class Stamp Here

Romantic Marriage #2 (1950)

I knew then that it couldn't go on like this. It was going to be his mother or our marriage, and I decided on a showdown....

"Once before I asked you to make a choice, Peter. I'm asking you again. Your mother's possessiveness is killing our marriage—killing our love. I'm not staying here another night. Are you coming with me—or are you staying with her?"

The slamming of the door behind him sounded like the death knell to my marriage, and fighting to choke back my tears, I began to pack. His mother had won. When I looked up and saw her standing in the doorway gloating, I wasn't too surprised....

"So you thought you could take my boy away from me. As if I'd let a snip like you have him."

First Romance #7 (1951)

I collected men as some people collect stamps, and had them all neatly pasted in my album of memories! I
didn't care if my human trophies were stolen goods, or if I was their stumbling block on the way to the altar!
Like a true collector, I valued what was hard to get . . . and I got what I wanted! One man never meant anything
to me but to serve as part of my collector's pattern. I had a scientific method for stealing hearts until that day
when I found I had no formula to mend my own!

FROM BOY LOVES GIRL, GIRL LOVES BOY · PANTHEON BOOKS · ED. MICHAEL BARSON · COMPILATION AND NEW TEXT © 1992 BY MICHAEL BARSON

My Personal Problem #3 (1958)

I am twenty-five years old now and my name is still **Miss** Joan Wilson. I work in a large office and that's about all I could say to describe my dull life.... Let's see ... what day is this? As though it matters.... Days and nights are all the same to me!

Love Lessons #4 (1950)

I knew now that Mike would never believe I was anything more than a common pick-up. After that, Lorna and Mike went by almost every evening, laughing and having good times, while I had to endure seeing it. Every time I thought that could be me with Mike—if only I had waited to be properly introduced! Oh—I was such a fool!

"'Yes, teen-agers, take heed to Beth's story. If a boy really wants to meet you, he'll do it without whistling from a corner, or some similar crude and distasteful way. Remember, a quick 'pick up' often means a fast 'let-down'!'"

FROM BOY LOVES GIRL, GIRL LOVES BOY · PANTHEON BOOKS · ED. MICHAEL BARSON · COMPILATION AND NEW TEXT © 1992 BY MICHAEL BARSON

Teen-Age Romances #38 (1954)

"Before we go to 'Dance Land,' this driver is going to collect his fare."
"How much do you charge, driver?"

Suddenly I understood it all. Kirk had dated me, hoping to find within me the same wild abandon that had attracted so many men to Ginger. . . .

"The same amount the passenger back there is paying."
"Sorry, Kirk. . . I can't afford that much. This passenger isn't paying up."

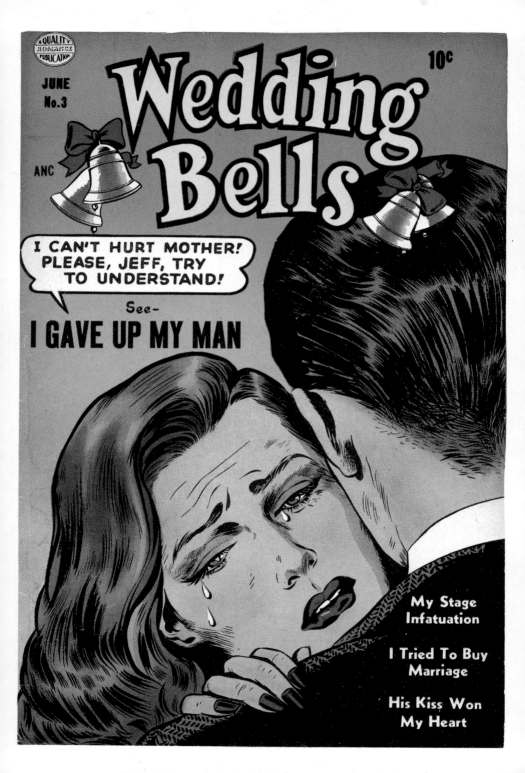

FROM BOY LOVES GIRL, GIRL LOVES BOY · PANTHEON BOOKS · ED. MICHAEL BARSON · COMPILATION AND NEW TEXT © 1992 BY MICHAEL BARSON

Wedding Bells #3 (1954)

My jubilation transmitted itself to my work, and at the fashion school I designed dresses as gay, as frothy as my heart! But, as days went by without word from Jeff, bands of misery closed about my heart. . . .

"He's forgotten me! All his talk of love . . . They were lies! (sob)"

"Forget him, dear! The best cure for a broken heart is work—think only of your career now! That's all that matters now . . . your career!"

"You're right, Mother! Just as you were right about Jeff!"

FROM BOY LOVES GIRL, GIRL LOVES BOY · PANTHEON BOOKS · ED. MICHAEL BARSON · COMPILATION AND NEW TEXT © 1992 BY MICHAEL BARSON

True-to-Life Romances #9 (1950)

"Oh, you dear, dear lovely dope! I'm going to kiss you!"

"Bruce Hecker, don't you dare!"

But Bruce was impetuous and forceful. I knew I would be kissed even before his lips touched mine.... When I found myself alone I think I hated Bruce more than I ever had before....

"Oh, why did Bruce do it? (Sob) Why? Why did I let him kiss me? I hate him, yet I allowed him to place his lips on mine, even while Fred's kiss was (sob) fresh in my memory!"

FROM BOY LOVES GIRL, GIRL LOVES BOY · PANTHEON BOOKS · ED. MICHAEL BARSON · COMPILATION AND NEW TEXT © 1992 BY MICHAEL BARSON

Diary Secrets #12 (1950)

Suddenly she was in my arms ... a smoldering ember of burning passion. My lips met hers in the most delicious, most strength-draining kiss I had ever experienced....

"It was fate that brought us together, Nikki! Fate! Say you'll marry me.... Please ..."

"Yes, Lee, I'll marry you! Just as soon as my contract is finished at the Golden Peacock! But I warn you, I have expensive tastes!"

LOVERS' LANE

NEVER BEFORE
A LOVE COMIC
LIKE THIS!

PDC

OCT. NO. 29

10¢

DAN WAS WAITING FOR ME TO DENY THE WHOLE STORY — TO CLEAR MYSELF. COULD I GO ON LYING TO HIM, PRETENDING . . . ?

I LONGED FOR HIS KISSES — I FELT MYSELF TREMBLE AS I LEANED AGAINST HIM, WANTING HIS LOVE, NEEDING IT . . .

"DON'T YOU LOVE ME?" I ASKED. "YOU DON'T ACT LIKE IT . . ."

MY HEART WHISPERED A SILENT PLEA — "DON'T QUESTION ME ANY MORE — DON'T MAKE ME LIE TO YOU . . ."

FROM BOY LOVES GIRL, GIRL LOVES BOY · PANTHEON BOOKS · ED. MICHAEL BARSON · COMPILATION AND NEW TEXT © 1992 BY MICHAEL BARSON

Lovers' Lane #29 (1952)

"The girl in this lingerie ad, Nina, bears a striking resemblance to you! A lot of my friends have called my attention to other ads. You evidently have been posing for that man—and very undignified poses. I'm sorry, but I don't want those kind of pictures of my future wife flooding the magazines. I think we've both made a mistake and had better call off our wedding plans."

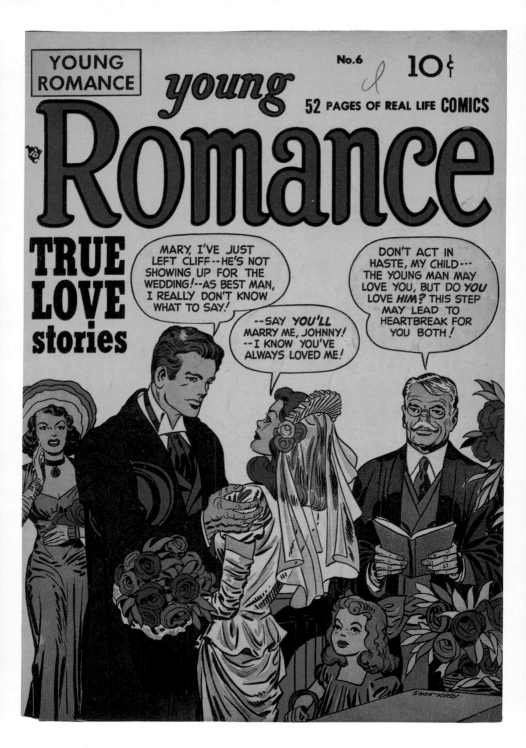

FROM BOY LOVES GIRL, GIRL LOVES BOY · PANTHEON BOOKS · ED. MICHAEL BARSON · COMPILATION AND NEW TEXT © 1992 BY MICHAEL BARSON

Young Romance #6 (1948)

"There—now you belong to me!"

"It . . . it was over so fast. . . . I don't feel married, really! . . . Where are we going now? The Summet Hotel! Why are we stopping here?"

"I thought we could register here! We certainly should have some kind of honeymoon."

"No! Take me home right away, Dennis! I want to go home!"

"You're acting like a child! What's the matter with you? There's nothing wrong in our going to a hotel together! We're married!"

PICTORIAL Romances

ANC 10¢

No. 10

They said it was wild folly and dangerous to do the things that I did...just for a chance to become a starlet.

Then it happened...and I had to stand by, knowing the awful truth, as my sister walked down the aisle.

HAVE A GOOD TIME, MARY. DON'T WORRY ABOUT ANYTHING!

I WILL, DEAR! KEEP YOUR EYE ON HIM, JEAN. YOU'RE THE ONLY WOMAN I TRUST WITH MY HUSBAND!

YOU INSIPID, LITTLE FOOL! BY THE TIME YOU GET BACK YOU WON'T HAVE A HUSBAND!

I WAS THE "OTHER WOMAN"

Pictorial Romances #10 (1951)

"Don't you see, Jim. Darling! I did it for us . . . so we could be together. . . . Just you and I!"

"You and I?! What a thick-headed fool I was not to have seen through you! Can't you get it through your head that I love my wife . . . and I always will! Why don't you find someone else to chase?"

"Why . . . you . . . you . . . And after all the business I threw your way!"

52
PAGES

SEPT
OCT

DARLING

ROMANCE

10¢ *Real Stories of* **TRUE LOVE**

AHC

NIKKI warned me that she would teach me a brand of love I had never known before— but she didn't warn me she had no heart! No soul! That it would destroy me as it had destroyed every other man. How I resolved this is told in "I WAS A VICTIM OF GIRL GLAM-OUR."

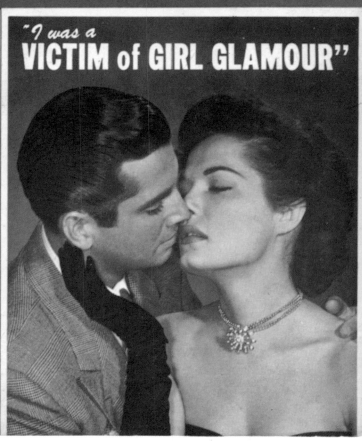

"I was a **VICTIM of GIRL GLAMOUR"**

Darling

FROM BOY LOVES GIRL, GIRL LOVES BOY · PANTHEON BOOKS · ED. MICHAEL BARSON · COMPILATION AND NEW TEXT © 1992 BY MICHAEL BARSON

Darling Romances #6 (1950)

While waiting for the trial I had time to think, and I realized that I had never actually loved Nikki.... That she had been a cancerous, irresistible disease with the power to hypnotize and destroy.... Not to love! One day.....

"You're so sweet, Vivian! So.... so gentle and good! I... I... don't deserve your love!"

"What's done is done, Lee. We'll just forget that this ever happened!"

And so my life began anew. But even in my wildest affairs with Nikki I had never dreamed of such love, such everlasting devotion as I have found with sweet Vivian! May God strike me dead if I ever again do anything or say anything to put more scars on her tender heart!

Exciting Stories of Young Love

TRUE·TO·LIFE

MAR / APR
K 10¢ 10
NO. 3

ROMANCES

TRUE TO LIFE ROMANCES

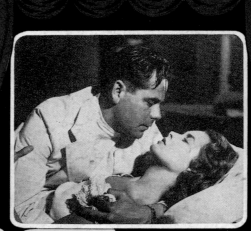

WHY DON'T YOU EVER SHOW ME SUCH TENDERNESS?

BECAUSE I DON'T BELIEVE IN DISPLAYS OF EMOTION!

"LOVE IN HEADLINES"
"HOLIDAY FROM HONOR"
"MONOTONOUS"
"ONE NIGHT ON A DATE"

PLUS

THE TRUE LIFE STORIES OF
GLENN FORD
AND
JANET LEIGH
M.G.M. STARS

True-to-Life Romances # 3 (1950)

"Jerry, y-you mean . . ."
"Uh-huh . . . looks like you haven't got any other boyfriends . . . and at your age, it's about time you started worrying about being an old maid! I might as well be the guy as anybody else!"

Men express affection in varied and sometimes peculiar ways . . . the **cavemen** *showed their love by beating their women—* **Eskimos** *rub noses—Jerry isn't that demonstrative but, I'm sure he loves me as deeply as any Casanova!*

MY PRIVATE LIFE
ANC
FEB. 10c
CHEAP... AM I?
"MEN DIDN'T RESPECT ME"
MY FRIENDSHIP CLUB AFFAIR • I SLAVED FOR HIM
HE KNEW MY SECRET

FROM BOY LOVES GIRL, GIRL LOVES BOY · PANTHEON BOOKS · ED. MICHAEL BARSON · COMPILATION AND NEW TEXT © 1992 BY MICHAEL BARSON

My Private Life #16 (1950)

"Why, you conceited dope! You've made a fool out of me long enough. I never want to see you again, Harry Bolton, much less date you."

"Not so fast, Honey! If you're not careful, I'll fix it so no one will ever date you again. Just a few little remarks here and there and your reputation will be null and void. Better think it over, Sweet."

I LOVED NOT WISELY BUT TOO WELL

ANC

Diary Secrets

ST. JOHN
TRADEMARK

THAT'S ELAINE GLEASON! SHE HAS AN APARTMENT IN NEW YORK, AND WHAT A LOT OF STORIES THEY TELL ABOUT THE WILD LIFE SHE'S BEEN LEADING THERE!

Our frenzied love reached its climax the day of the hot-rod derby...

Can a man with a roving eye be a good husband? Eric was waiting for my answer.

No. 14
TEN CENTS

FROM BOY LOVES GIRL, GIRL LOVES BOY · PANTHEON BOOKS · ED. MICHAEL BARSON · COMPILATION AND NEW TEXT © 1992 BY MICHAEL BARSON

Diary Secrets #14 (1952)

I was a young eager girl, living in fascinating Greenwich Village, ready to conquer New York! The neighbors and townfolk snubbed me completely. Several times I heard them whispering behind my back. A girl who had her own little apartment in New York and who aspired to something more than doing household chores or working in a cannery didn't conform to their standards. . . . .

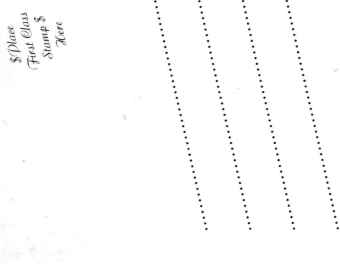

FROM BOY LOVES GIRL, GIRL LOVES BOY · PANTHEON BOOKS · ED. MICHAEL BARSON · COMPILATION AND NEW TEXT © 1992 BY MICHAEL BARSON

True Life Secrets #23 (1954)

At five I got what I wanted by screaming and kicking. At sixteen my methods of getting what I wanted were less violent but just as cruel.

"Faith, dear, here's a box of candy for you."

"Well, you can just keep it.... If I can't have that fur coat, you needn't try to bribe me with candy."

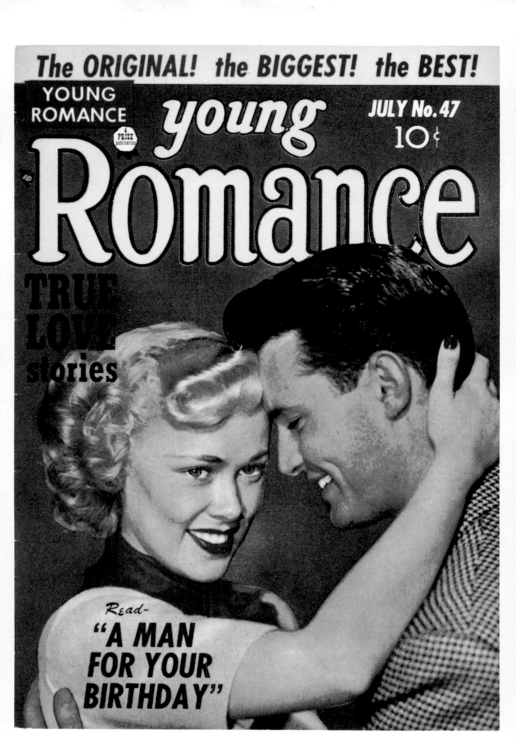

FROM BOY LOVES GIRL, GIRL LOVES BOY · PANTHEON BOOKS · ED. MICHAEL BARSON · COMPILATION AND NEW TEXT © 1992 BY MICHAEL BARSON

Young Romance #47 (1952)

Spoiled or not, I did want love! What woman doesn't? But to Dad, love was just a word!

"Love! Bah! Love and marriage are a business, a partnership! A clever person shops around until he finds the best buy . . . and buys it! Finding a husband is no different!"

"Except that you can't buy a man!"

"Why not? Mona, why don't we go shopping for a man for you? If that's what you want. . . . I've got a dozen bright young men working for me! Come down . . . pick one out, and I'll present him to you as a birthday gift! Why not?"

"Why . . . I don't know any reason why not! Nothing will come out of it, of course, but . . . it might be fun, at that!"

FROM BOY LOVES GIRL, GIRL LOVES BOY · PANTHEON BOOKS · ED. MICHAEL BARSON · COMPILATION AND NEW TEXT © 1992 BY MICHAEL BARSON

Teen-Age Romances #25 (1952)

During the first few months, I really enjoyed the baby and forgot about the gang. But gradually the routine of caring for him, fixing formulas and idling around the apartment while he was napping began to wear on my nerves. I longed for my past diversion.... Yes, Jackie was cute.... but it seemed so unjust that I should be tied down! Was all the fun in life over so soon for me? So much is going on outside while I sit here. I'm too young to be shut up like this!

FROM BOY LOVES GIRL, GIRL LOVES BOY · PANTHEON BOOKS · ED. MICHAEL BARSON · CCMPILATION AND NEW TEXT © 1992 BY MICHAEL BARSON

True Love Confessions #10 (1955)

I was the daughter of wealth and indulgence! Only the best clothes, the most exclusive school, the richest boyfriends were good enough for me! Was it any wonder that when the financial roof came crashing around my family, I was unprepared? Especially since I had dated the best "catch" in our circles. The sudden disaster of poverty filled me with shame! How furious I was when a mere garage mechanic tried to date me! It took a hard jolt to make me understand true values . . . and recognize my own **False Values of Love!**

My Lips Yearned For His Kisses ... I WAS A LONELY WAR BRIDE
ANC
Romantic MARRIAGE
ST. JOHN
No. 23
TEN CENTS
ASLEEP AGAIN! I KNOW THIS JOB KEEPS ME OUT PRETTY LATE, BUT THE LEAST HE COULD DO IS WAIT UP FOR ME. MAYBE MOTHER WAS RIGHT...HOW CAN A MARRIAGE SURVIVE WITHOUT ANY COMPANIONSHIP?
In this issue:
Torn Between Marriage and Career...
WHITE COLLAR WIFE
MY OWN WORST ENEMY

FROM BOY LOVES GIRL, GIRL LOVES BOY · PANTHEON BOOKS · ED. MICHAEL BARSON · COMPILATION AND NEW TEXT © 1992 BY MICHAEL BARSON

Romantic Marriage #23 (1954)

Work at the office kept piling up, taking most of my time and energy!

"Marge, what happened to my shirts? I need a fresh one . . . got to see a client today. . . . "

"Oh, Charlie, the laundry was closed when I got home, so—"

"I don't want to hear another word about your job! I don't want to see any of the money you're making! I'm sick of the whole business!"

"Darling, it's only for a little while, *believe me!*"

"Your 'little while' is long enough to have turned our marriage into a joke! We don't have a home any more, Marge . . . you've ruined it!"